PROCESSED FOR THE PROMISE: FINALLY I FOUND REAL LOVE

By Natakey Page Owens

Copyright Page

Natakey Page Owens. © 2019

ISBN: 978-0-578-48050-3
Editors: P31 Publishing, LLC
For more information, please visit www.natakeypage.com

Because of the dynamic nature of the internet, any web addresses or links contained in this book may have changed since publication and may no longer be valid.The views expressed in this work are solely those of the author and do not necessarily reflect the views of the publisher, and the publisher disclaims any responsibility for them.

Printed in the United States of America

Photo credit: Bernard McPhatter
Makeup Artist: Valerie Barr

Table of Contents

Acknowledgments

I want to take the time to thank my Heavenly Father, who strengthened me throughout this process, especially when I did not think I could do it.

My children whom I love with all of me. They believed in me and encouraged me to the very end.

To Michele and Crystal, you girls really rock! Thank you for never judging me even when I probably sounded crazy, but that was just my faith increasing.

To My Fierce and Fearless GSisters who held me accountable for what I said I wanted to do. You helped me to believe in myself, learn that it is okay not to be okay, to ask for help if I need it, know that true genuine women who want to see you succeed does exist, and most of all did not judge me based on my past.

Finally, to all those who I asked to cover me throughout my writing process, because you prayed for me, I went through the fire and came out without a burn.

Endorsements

ow!! Toc you did it!! Congratulations!! I am so proud of you! We've been BFF forever and ever (since 8th grade). I have seen you conquer so many things throughout this journey and you didn't give yourself much credit either! Now others get to read your first book and we will give you the credit that you so deserve. You are amazing!! I've seen where you could have given up from the hard times you had from lack of love in relationships, through family and friendships, but you survived it and you are still thriving!! Through your transparency, this book is going to be absolutely outstanding. Continue to let your light shine and blossom like the butterfly you are!! Everything is a process and I've seen you transform from the caterpillar to this beautiful butterfly and now you are soaring. I've seen you grow in faith and that has given me hope for myself as well. You have been my friend, my prayer partner, my ear, my head to head, my sister from another mother, my home girl, my ace-coon-boom and you have always been there! I'll like to take the time to say congratulations in conquering one of the many accomplishments your heart desires. This book is going to be just the beginning of others discovering how amazing you are. I know your kids are super proud of you because you have demonstrated to them that the circumstances of your past (or right now) does not have to affect your flow and or your future. Playing many roles in their life may have seem tough from time to time, but you knew your "Why". You are an awesome mom and my best friend so DO NOT dim your light for anyone or anything....someone else needs that shine of hope in their life! You ROCK.... Love ya Chica!

Michele Drewery

I met Natakey in the fifth grade and she became a sister to me. For the first time I had someone to share my secrets and someone to sit in the park with and laugh aimlessly about absolutely nothing. Natakey has always been there to lend her shoulder when I needed it. Watching my best friend undergo such an amazing transition reminds me of what a butterfly goes through. The transition of a butterfly is such an amazing process to watch. Think about it, when we look at a caterpillar we do not think twice about its beauty. On the surface we don't see it right away, but after the butterfly breaks from its cocoon we are marvelled at its beauty. Especially the different patterns and the colors. It's the same thing with Natakey, I have been blessed to see her transition out of her cocoon and blossom into a beautiful woman of God. I am even more amazed with her relationship with him and how she is allowing him to use her through this book! I am honored to call her my friend and most importantly my sister in Christ. I can't wait to see the amazing things God is going to do in her life from here. Be blessed my friend!

Crystal Davis

Introduction

Hey there! The fact that you have taken the time to read my book is already a blessing. God allowed me to suffer a while so that he could restore me. He presented me with this title and I was unsure about how I was going to actually write a book (Haha, yeah right). Well.....guess what? He did it! Yes, he did it for little ole me. I am truly grateful and honored for all he has done for me over this last year. Who would have ever thought that this single mother of three, who has many imperfections, who is a domestic violence survivor, who once had low self-esteem, who once attempted suicide (but thought about it plenty of times), suffered from anxiety, abandonment, and rejection; yet God saw fit to use me anyway (Praise break!). I am purposed filled and willing to be used by God. He is allowing me to share my story with those who have been searching for love in all the wrong places.

Because I feared being judged by others, I am reminded in Isaiah 41:10 ESV "Fear not, for I am with you; do not be dismayed, for I am your God. I will strengthen you, I will help you, I will uphold you with my righteous right hand". My faith had to be bigger than my fear so that I could be used to my full potential. It is my hope to reach many women all over the world, but if I reach only ONE, I believe that God will be pleased with me.

Get ready! Keep an open heart and mind as I take you through my process of finding real love. I had to surrender all, develop a close relationship with God, discover who I was, do some intentional self development, and now I await for what has been promised to me. Come on my sister, grab yourself a drink of your choice, and cuddle on your chair with a nice throw blanket. You good? Great! Let's begin the process.

Chapter 1

Surrender All

Transformation happens on the other side of surrender

$\mathcal{S}$ urrender. Yes. That's exactly what it took for me, giving up being in control. It is what I had to do when my life seemed to be too strenuous to handle. I didn't know which direction to go in. Have you ever felt this way? Like you were just tired of not knowing what direction to take? As if you keep going in the same direction, but hoping that you will end up in a new place. You are aware that this is considered insanity. Boy, was I insane. I've lived my life without knowing what true love was and because I didn't know what it was, I found myself in many unfulfilled relationships. I wanted to be loved to the point of trying to make someone love me. At some point in my life, I had to decide that I could no longer do that; therefore, I had to surrender it all. You're probably thinking surrender all to who? Well, let me take you back to two of the most memorable relationships that

I had. There have been a few, but to me there are two that truly changed my life.

In 1998, my eyes brought my attention to this tall, slim, curly haired guy. How many of you know that looks can be very deceiving? Well, a friend girl and I followed him to give him my number. Things moved really quickly between us. I was pregnant after only four months of 'talking". Shortly after, the abuse started.

One night in particular, I was at home lightly sleeping, when I was awakened by a loud voice and the smell of alcohol over me. Other than the fact that he had been drinking, I am still unaware of what had him so angry. This anger that he was feeling caused him to pick an argument and led to him choking me. I grabbed ahold of his wrist trying to get him to let go of my neck. I could hardly breathe. He then quickly grabbed me by my hair and slammed me to the floor. I was four months pregnant with his child. Can you imagine the pain that I felt while lying on the floor holding my stomach, in tears and very scared? I began crying out to God to please let my daughter be okay. I was in disbelief of what happened. What did I do to deserve him being so malicious towards me and our unborn child?

I didn't have enough confidence to leave him after that; therefore, more abusive days followed for four more years. Not only was I allowing myself to be abused physically, but emotionally and verbally also. I stayed hoping that things would change. Nothing changed until I decided to call on my heavenly

Father, hoping He would hear me and really know that it was truly coming from my heart this time. The prayer went like this: "Lord, if this is not the man for me, please remove him from my life and give me the strength to go on. I can not do this on my own."

You do know that sometimes God will answer prayers speedily and then some times He will take awhile. This particular time He came quickly, and I do believe He was looking down at me saying " I was waiting on you to just ask." I am reminded of the scripture:

"Ask and it will be given to you; seek, and you will find; knock, and it will be opened to you. For everyone who asks receives; and the one who seeks finds; and the one who knocks, it will be opened."(Matthew 7: 7-8 ESV) I am so grateful to have finally asked to be released from that toxic relationship.

I allowed this to happen because I had 'daddy issues'. Those issues consisted of low self-esteem, rejection, abandonment, and lack of love. A lot of my decision making was based on generational curses, which I will discuss with you later.

Clearly the abuse was not love, but I was willing to settle because I did not know anything different. However, I believe that we have two deeper inner voices. It is called your flesh and your spirit. Your spirit voice is what helps you to make 'good godly decisions'. My spirit inner voice gave me enough strength to call out to God, but my flesh voice, which desires to do things that are ungodly, was still trying to be in control. I went from being released from one toxic relationship to another relationship years later that had 'POTENTIAL' (so I thought).

If we do not allow ourselves some time to really heal after coming out of an abusive relationship, we will enter into another relationship with unforgiveness, mistrust, bitterness, and a lot of extra baggage. Aren't you tired of pulling bags everywhere you go? And they keep pulling you down or slowing you down from receiving your best. If you continue with this pattern, the next relationship will now have the potential to become abusive or just be full of dysfunction. Please allow yourself to take time to get to know *who* you are. In my case, I was going from one relationship to the next without taking the time to HEAL. Which leads me to share with you the story of the trooper.

I have been a licensed cosmetologist for twenty years and the shop consist of both stylist and barbers. You know all kinds of men come through the door. Short, tall, skinny, fat, wide, narrow(ha ha you get the point). I always speak to everyone that comes in even if I do not get a full look at them. There was a barber that worked behind me and he would cut some really attractive men's hair, but the majority of them were related to him and very light skinned. Now, I do not want you to believe that I am color struck because I am not. But let me keep it *100* with you, I prefer a nice dark skinned guy with pretty teeth. Yes, we can have a preference.

There was this guy that I noticed a few times when he came in to get his haircut. He was probably about 5'9 or 5'10, brown skinned with a mustache, was nicely built as if maybe he worked out on a regular. One day, I get up enough nerve to inquire about him to my coworker. He asked him a few questions, one being if he had a girlfriend. The answer to that was he had a FRIEND. That should have been my cue to leave it right there, but because he did not say that he had a girlfriend per se, I proceeded with giving him my number.

Have you ever had warning signs but chose to ignore them? The thought of having someone in your life really loving you was just more important than that minor situation. The thought of maybe he will let the other person go and make you the main girl, or you were just so patient that you would hang around to see him change. He made it clear that he does not want to be committed. Somehow though, he would want to do things that committed couples do, but only at his convenience. Depending on how he felt you might sometimes be able to hang out in public and get a few gifts.

I definitely saw the provider in him but he was completely emotionally disconnected. The funny thing is that he did admit that to me, but for whatever reason I still chose to hold on the the potential that I saw in him and us becoming official. Guess what? It did not happened. God decided to shake it up to the point that he would bring the relationship to a pause and I would have to totally surrender the relationship to Him.

Have you ever seen the movie *War Room*? If not, I highly recommend that you do. This movie totally changed my life. I finally learned how to really pray. I knew to pray when things were going bad, but seem to forget about being grateful in the happy moments. We must learn to pray without ceasing. 1 Thessalonians 5:17-18 ESV says:" pray without ceasing, give thanks in all circumstances; for this is the will of God in Christ Jesus for you." I began learning God's word so that I could call him back what he said, plus be able to do it through the good and the bad.

This particular day after finally being tired of being ignored (text messaging is the worst), crying and asking what's wrong with me, I fell to my knees with my face buried into the floor and cried out AGAIN to God and said, "Father, I am tired. I am tired of all these dead relationships. Giving my body to them and they really do not want ME. I totally surrender to you. Please forgive me. Teach me how to love and show me what it really looks like. I want to be able to feel it like others have describe it to me, yet I really did not understand how they were so in love with you. Tell me what to do and I will do it. Make me an example." After saying all this the Holy Spirit whispered to me, "Second chance. My way." This was the beginning of my process with learning how to love and to be loved. It has been very difficult, but worth it.

Our ways and thoughts are nothing compared to the ways and thoughts of God. He knows what is best for our lives. Our stories are designed to bring about purpose. The pain that we endure is processed so that it may fulfill the very thing that will bring about glory to God. He uses us as the vessel only if you are willing. Are you willing? Are you willing to share your story in hopes of it reaching others who have also experienced what you have? In hopes of giving others hope through your own testimony.

Surrendering to God was only the beginning of my process to finally finding real love. I am now on my way to building a close and intimate relationship with God. And when he sees fit to allow that special one to find me, I will be in a better space. A space of loving Him and loving who I am.

Chapter 2

Purge

If it doesn't nourish your soul, get rid of it

I have surrendered to God. Finally, I am no longer trying to do things my way. During this process I have asked him to teach me how to love and help me to be able to recognize that real feeling of love from Him. Well this is a process and it did not happen overnight for me. The next step was to gracefully break me. I do not mean literally to break me but, 1 Corinthians 5:17 says: "Therefore if any man be in Christ, he is a new creature; old things are passed away; behold, all things are become new". This meant that I had to let go of all the old things, and in order for this to happen, I had to be purged.

According to vocabulary.com dictionary, purge comes from the Latin word purgare, meaning purify. Impure things and thoughts had to be removed from me. This included the soul ties and the unbelief of being able to have a healthy godly relationship.

I definitely had to be purged in order for me to be used by God. 2 Timothy 2:21 ESV reads: "Therefore if anyone cleanses himself from what is dishonorable, he will be a vessel for honorable use, set apart as holy, useful for the master of the house, ready for every good work". Thank you Jesus. Being purged from past relationships and unhealthy soul ties now allows God to fully use me to do his Kingdom work.

Remember the last relationship I mentioned to you? Yes, the guy from the barbershop. Did I also mention that he is the one that I really believed that I truly loved? How did I know this? This time instead of me jumping into another relationship, I told God that I would trust Him with the relationship. I began to pray for him. The Holy Spirit did say that I had a second chance, but I had to do it His way. You are probably wondering the same thing I was wondering. Is the second chance with this guy? I am not sure, but the fact that I am learning to trust God with everything; I have to trust that if it is or isn't him, I will be very satisfied.

Okay, back to me being purged. So, this last relationship was definitely a sexual relationship therefore there was a strong soul tie. A soul tie is like a linkage in the soul realm between two people. This soul tie can be both negative and positive. You can also have an emotional soul tie to someone, which make break ups harder. Some people have the gift of "goodbye", but I do not. I constantly had this guy on my mind. When I woke up, all throughout the day, and at bedtime - he was on my mind. I was constantly asking God to help me not to think about him so much. Again, it was a strong soul tie. I honestly felt like I was having some type of withdrawal, and it did not feel good at all.

The positive side of having a soul tie is through a godly marriage or true healthy friendships. Matthew 19:5 ESV "And therefore a shall man shall leave his father and his mother, and hold fast to his wife: and the two shall be one flesh." The purpose of this healthy soul tie is to build a fruitful and strong relationship between the man and woman. God's intention for sex is only for those who are married. Period. Because we live in a fallen world, we are capable of being conformed to its worldly ways. Sex outside of marriage is considered an unhealthy soul tie. This is why you tend to still have feelings for that ex-lover. You just can't seem to get him out of your thoughts.The worst part of that is everyone you have had sex with and they have had sex with, you both are having sex with them. Can you imagine all of those different spirits on the inside of you? This is one of the reasons your emotions are all over the place. Sex was also designed to enjoy but it must be done in the proper order. This is really pleasing to God.

My last sexual encounter with Trooper was a very scary one. After the fact, I returned home and took a nap. When I decided to get up, I could not move. I felt this really strong hold on me, as if someone was literally holding me down. It made me feel like I was depressed. I tried to get up again, but was only able to lift my head up for a quick second. I just did not have the energy to get up. What is happening to me? I do not know this to be exact, but in my heart, I do believe that he may have been depressed and the spirit had entered into my body. Yes, just like that. Eventually, the feeling lifted off of me. That day forward I promised myself and God that I would no longer give my body away being unmarried.

I have gone months before without having sex. The longest time was one year but it was not about intentionally waiting until marriage. I just was not involved with anyone so I was not having sex. This time was different, I intentionally asked God to give me self control over my body. That meant I could not masturbate either, because I would be sinning against my own body. The bible says " I appeal to you therefore, brothers, by the mercies of God, to present your bodies as a living sacrifice, holy and acceptable to God, which is your spiritual worship". Romans 12:1 ESV This was a struggle for me.

I was having one of those days. I had worked all day and my hormones were 'on one hundred'. I wanted to have sex so bad that I had to go straight home, get in my bed in a fetal position, pull the covers over my head and cry. Here again, I was learning to trust God while he was breaking me away from the impurities of this soul tie to rebuild me into the woman I was destined to be. I was also learning how to deny my flesh. You do know that I still have those moments because I am human and I am not a virgin (eyes rolling up in my head). You know that you can be kept by God if you desire to be kept? I highly recommend that you allow yourself to be purged from any impurities that could be blocking you from getting all that God has for your life. I had to recognize what my triggers were. I could not watch any sexual scenes on television, could not have any extra drinks, especially by myself. Honey, this was extremely difficult and I still have days that are challenging!

After reading *Sexless Single*, by Jill Bulluck, I purchased a promise ring to remind myself that I am waiting on God to release my husband to find and pursue me. In the meantime, I am still learning to love and be loved faithfully by God . I can proudly say as of October 18, 2018, I have been abstinent for three years! Can I get a hallelujah?(thank you Jesus for keeping me) Can I please get a high five? Not only did I have to stop having sex, but I had to isolate myself for a few months.

Isolation is not all bad. I was not depressed, God wanted all of my attention. Isolation gave me time to really develop that relationship I needed with God. I was not hanging out at all. Yep, I am saved, love the Lord and from time to time I still like to go out to an event that is not a church event. (Fix your face. It is okay. Just know your own convictions)

For a while my routine was working, workout three days a week and church. During this time I was still in my weak stage and very frail. You have to recognize your own weaknesses and confess them to God so that He will give you the strength you need to get through your tough moments. I had plenty of them and still do. But God.

Being content living in an unhealthy way is not what God has planned for your life. You will have to allow him to purge you from those impurities, be willing to let go of whatever is keeping you from your best, so you can be processed to receive the abundance of love from God. Once this happens you can begin to rebuild from brokeness.

After trooper returned from overseas, I shared with him where I was spiritually. He basically was not where I was, and the relationship slowly drifted apart. Let's stop right here for one second and pray:

Father, as you begin to rebuild this beautiful woman, I pray that she is open to learning how to love You, herself, and then others. There is no way that she can do this without you. Purge her from all impurities and allow the Holy Spirit to assure her that she is worthy, she is enough, and she is worth the wait. There is more to her than just her body and her past mistakes. Continue to take her through this process, as she embraces her truth. Let her be open to accept all the good and the bad. I believe that in the end she will see that it was all worth it. In Jesus' name, Amen

Chapter 3

Developing an Intimate Relationship

You know the very relationship that I so desired to have with a man, is what I really should have been desiring to have with the main Man, God. God is a jealous God, and he does not want anybody or anything before him. If you do this, it is called idolatry. Idolatry is when a person has extreme admiration, love, or reverence for something or someone. This idol then will have some great control over your emotions and decisions.

Do you know the story of Moses leading the Israelites out of Egypt? While Moses was up on the mountain, Aaron decides to help them make a god because they did not know what happened to Moses. Aaron agreed and asked them to remove all their gold jewelry, which he then created a gold calf. The Israelites began to worship this calf. This caused God to be very angry and he was about to destroy them. Moses asked that God would have favor over the Israelites, and He did.(Exodus 32: 1-14) I honestly believe that Jesus interceded for me, because I did not know any better. Oh, but how grateful I am to have been raised up by a praying grandmother. I believe she took it to Jesus and Jesus took it to God, and he agreed to have mercy and favor on me too. She definitely planted the foundation for me.

At the age of 12, I accepted Christ in my life. I remembered going to church with my grandmother on first and third Sundays. And on second and fourth Sundays we would only have Sunday School. Yes, I was raised up in a Baptist church. Do you know anything about that Baptist upbringing? Well, at this Baptist Church, when you did decide to make Christ the head of your life, at the invitation hour, they would place a chair or chairs up front, and you would walk up there and sit in the chair. The pastor would then say: and if you confess with your mouth the Lord Jesus and believe in your heart that God has raised Him from the dead, you will be saved. For with the heart one believes unto righteousness, and with the mouth confession is made unto salvation. (Romans 10: 9-10) So in a nutshell, what saves you is the fact that you believe. That is exactly what I did, I believed. The only thing here is that I was not told about the relationship that I needed to build with God along with me believing. As I look back on it, it was totally okay though. In 1 Corinthians 13: 11 says, "When I was a child, I spoke as a child, I understood as a child, I thought as a child; but when I became a (wo) man, I put away childish things".

You remember me telling you how I finally surrendered my life to Christ after the last relationship I had? I was now 38 years old. That is 26 years later after I accepted Christ in my life. Yes, and you best believe I went through a lot of things. Some of it was just bad decisions and some of it was just life. Either way, I was ready to build that relationship with God. The first thing I learned was how to pray. Not just when things were challenging but also when it was going smooth. I would wake up early read a devotion and pray. You know when I would pray, I would do it as if He and I were having a conversation. If I was upset, I told him (even though He already knew), if I was confused or just excited, I would share it all. I began googling scriptures that I needed for that particular season of my life. I needed to learn how to trust God.

Have you ever been there? Not knowing how to fully trust God? You would treat Him as if He was like the other men in your life. The fact that I have been let down by other men so many times, I had the nerve to box God in with them. I recognized that, so I began to ask Him to help me to trust Him.

My youngest daughter was set to graduate in June of 2017, it was May and she had been accepted to all the schools she had applied to, but had not made a decision on where she wanted to go to college. I was already nervous about being an empty nester, and she was taking forever to make her decision, which was making my nerves worse. I was asking on a regular basis now, "uhm Pooh, have you decided what you are going to do?" Her response, "No." And it was very nonchalant. Honestly, she did not seem to be worried about it either. I continued to pray and ask God to help me trust Him. I had wrote in my journal about my daughter making a decision on her college choice and that she would receive scholarship money, especially because I had a son already attending college. Three weeks before graduation, (praise break, as I think about His goodness) my daughter received $84,000 in scholarship money for over a four year period for academics and athletics. Honey, tell me He won't do it! Yes He will. That was the beginning of me learning how to really trust him. When I find myself doubting again in other situations, I just ask him again to help me trust Him.

Having a relationship with God is an absolute must. Desiring other relationships is fine but it can not take the place of the relationship that you have with God. There is one sure thing with this relationship, and that is He will always be there for you no matter what!!!!!! The more time that you spend with him praying and reading his word you begin to learn more about his ways. You will be able to hear Him speak to you when you are about to make a bad decision. You will be capable of listening for his whisper, when he is giving you directions that relates to your process of discovering who you are. As I began to learn more about God, I had to understand that everything would work out, if I continued to trust and believe Him. Things were about to shake up as He moved me to the next phase of my process. It was now time to gracefully break me to rebuild me into the woman I am to be.

Chapter 4

♥♥

Who Are You?

If you want to be happy, you must be true to who you are

So far you have surrendered, been gracefully broken through purging, had a healthy isolation period, and now it's time to be gracefully rebuilt into the woman you were meant to be. You start by first discovering who you are. What is your true identity? I read a quote that says: "The greatest challenge in life is discovering who you are. The second greatest is being happy with what you find." Yes, the good, the bad, and the ugly.

As for me, I am a young woman who struggled with low self-esteem, had little confidence, no self love, and had issues with comparing myself to other women. None of the things I just named were noticeable. This is something I struggled with on the inside of me. Do you have some of those same issues, but only you know it? You would be embarrassed to admit to others that you do not love yourself, or that you have low self-esteem issues. Well, don't be because you and I are definitely not alone. The first step to recovering from anything is admitting you have a problem.

My low self-esteem came from abusive relationships and abandonment issues from my father. The real me could not be in fear of what would happen later or it not being enough for them to stay around. I can recall a time when l was at a social gathering with the ex abuser and I was having a conversation with one of the guys there. I typically smile when I talk to people with no hidden agenda at all. I was laughing and talking just like everyone else was and I was sober. The abuser said nothing while we were there but once we got home all hell broke out. I was accused of liking the guy and told I was smiling too much. I was told that maybe I wanted to have sex with him since I was smiling so hard. I should be glad that he did not hit me in my face while we were sitting there. In my mind, it was a harmless conversation. I was aware of the fact that my man was right there in the same place and I would not have disrespected him in any way. However, the abuser's thoughts were different. Situations like this would cause me to look straight ahead and not have any conversations with other guys (especially if he was present). I had more sad expressions than I did happy ones. I did not love myself enough to remove myself from this dysfunction and it was starting to become the norm for me. But it was not who I was.

When I was eight years old, my dad divorced my mother and later remarried. He married someone who had three children from a previous relationship. Of course, this meant that he would have to take care of them as well. I honestly find nothing wrong with that. I fully understand that they all came together as a package deal. The issue was that he took care of them and not me. He was very inconsistent with calling me or coming to get me for the summer. There were times when he said he was coming and he never showed up. Not even a simple phone call to let me know that the plan had changed. When I loss my mother at the age of ten, he was not there to comfort me, love on me, and just to encourage me. My goodness, I had just loss my mother! That would have been a good time to have his love and support. He was unavailable to do that for me and because of that I had low self-esteem and trust issues. I also felt rejected, but there was still hope for me.

It takes courage and confidence to admit that our past have some control over who we are. Notice I said SOME, not ALL. There is always room to make changes in our life. The first thing you do is own it, and second you make the necessary adjustments. You will have to learn how to affirm yourself and not become what others say you are. Do not allow how others treat you to dictate who you are. You learn how to forgive and release any bitterness, which I will address later on with self development.

After the abuser left me, he moved on to the next. He moved quick with the relationship and was married again only a year and a few months after we were legally over. I thought that I was over the relationship until he actually got married. I began to question myself. What was wrong with me? What does she have that I don't have? Is she prettier? All kind of things were racing through my mind. Not only did the abuser move on quick, but so did the trooper. He had me believing that he was not ready for commitment, only to find out later he was now living with someone. That was a straight slap in my face and it really hurt. And once again I say Lord, what is wrong with me?

Comparing yourself to other women does not make you any better or any less than them. You are who you are. You should not put other women down to make you feel better about yourself. And please do not put yourself down either because that man may have decided to choose her instead of you. Guess what? Life goes on and you will be just fine. Now, pause right here for a minute and go listen to Mary J Blige's song *Just Fine*.......now turn it up! I like this part right here: *"feels so good, when you're doing all the things that you want to do Get the best out of life, treat yourself to something new Keep your head up high In yourself, believe in you, believe in me Having a really good time, I'm not complaining And I'm a still wear a smile if its raining I got to enjoy myself regardless I appreciate life, I'm so glad I got mine"* Yesssss, I love it. My life's just fine. Go turn the music back down and continue on with discovering who you are. You feeling real good right now, huh?

The spiritual side to all this is that God created you and I in His own image. Our identity is in him. He created us not man. Psalm 130:13-14 says,"For you formed my inward parts; you knitted me together in my mother's wound. I praise you, for I am fearfully and wonderfully made". Wonderful are your works; my soul knows it very well. Can you see the hope in these two verses? God created you. He knows the inside of you because he put you together while you were in your mother's womb. No man gets to determine who you are. The fact that you were created in God's likeness makes you one special lady. You will have to learn to see yourself the way God created you.

I can now say that my self esteem is higher, I am loving me some me, honey, and I do not care what others say or think. My confidence is growing daily, even as I write this chapter. I no longer compare myself to other women, but embrace the bold, beautiful and courageous woman that I am. I know you are special in your own way and I take nothing from you. I celebrate you. I am great at being me, and would be horrible at trying to be you. I own who I am and continue to make the necessary adjustments daily. You should, without question do the same.

Chapter 5

Where Are You From?

"No matter where you're from, your dreams are valid."
Lupita Nyong'o

Now that you have a discovered who you are, let's move on to where you are from. Knowing where you are from helps you to identify with why you do some of the things you do. The obvious here is that you come from God. He is the main source of your being, your joy, your peace, and your happiness. When he decided to create us in his own image, he created male and female. In Genesis it speaks about how God created Adam and Eve. Eve was created from Adam's rib, and Adam was created from dust that came from the ground. In my opinion, that makes us more special than men. The fact that you and I were not created from dirt we should not allow ourselves to be treated as such. You are the daughter of a king, therefore you are a beautiful princess.

God also made it so that male and female would be fruitful and multiply. Our parents came together (right or wrong) and produced us. You may have some of your mother's traits and some of your father's traits. I think I have more of my mother than my father. My life itself resembles my mother's almost identically. Before I tell you about just how much we share in common, I want you to think about both of your parents. Which one do you seem to have a lot in common with when it comes to some of the decisions that you have made in your life? These decisions can be good or bad.

As for me, my mother was very loyal and giving. She was loved by many. She would help anyone out if she could, and I am also this way. My mother also had three children, two girls and a boy. All of us had different fathers and she married one, which was my father. I told you earlier that they divorced when I was eight. She was a heroin addict which caused her not to be attentive to us. She was also co-dependent on men. At the age of twenty-nine her life was taken by the hands of her boyfriend. He stabbed her three times on the left side of her chest and one of the stabs pierced her heart. This has taught me that you can be here today and gone tomorrow.

I have three children, two girls and a boy. They all have different fathers, and I married one of them. I was in a domestic violence relationship and almost killed him. I am so grateful that I didn't. I would have been in prison and my child would have been without a father and my children, without a mother. Do you see the similarity here? I was born in a family with generational curses. I did not ask for this, but it was already a part of me. Similarly, Eve ate the apple which caused God to curse her, the serpent, and Adam. Thank God for Jesus. Reading Genesis 3 will give you more insight.

There are probably generational curses in your family too. Have you noticed a pattern with some of your family issues? I am sure in some families there may be a history of alcoholism, molestation, drugs, poverty, and more. You get the point. And yes, there are also some great things about your family too, but I am focusing on those things that may have a negative effect on why you may have a issue with loving yourself. This is where you come from, but it does not have to determine where you will go. Generational curses can be broken and it can start with you.

God revealed to me, as I was going through this process of learning how to love myself and be loved by a real Man, that I was the way I was because of the curse that was on my family. For example, not only did my mother and I experience abuse but so did her sister and mother. I decided that it will stop right here. Think about those curses that may have a stronghold over your life and let's begin to ask God to break the curse. Lets pray:

Father thank you for allowing us to see the generational curses that are upon us and giving us hope to know that it can be destroyed if we believe. We give you thanks that regardless of the family we were born in that you still have plans for our lives. Help us to accept the things that we cannot change and the strength to change the things we can. Continue to guide us as we trust in you with all our heart. In Jesus name. Amen

Chapter 6

Why Are You Here?

"God uses loss, betrayal, persecution, to force us to change.
He's not trying to make your life miserable,
He's pushing you into your purpose."

Does it feel good now that you have begun discovering who you are and where you are from? The next thing you have to do is ask yourself is why are you here? You do know that you are not here by accident? The fact that you *were* conceived is more important than *how* you were conceived. There is purpose in all of our lives. You were not just place on this earth just to work, go to school, to have children, to be married, go to church, to be mother, or to just to enjoy life. You were placed on earth to bring about glory to God. There are people who need to hear your story. Your pain is on purpose; to bring about a purpose. It will cause you to birth exactly what God had planned, if you are willing. Remember, he is a gentleman and he will not force you to do anything. You were created to be a success. Period. He doesn't want us to take this pain, suppress it, and not share it with others. There is someone who has experienced some of the same things that you have and can find some hope in you sharing your story.

I read a book during my time of isolation. I actually did a lot of reading during this time but one of the books in particular was *Understanding Your Potential* by Myles Munroe. He explains the reason for asking God why are you here. What did he create you to do? You already know that God had your story written out before you were conceived, but you do not know exactly how it will turn out. I do know that it will be victory for you and glory for God. He knows the appointed time and day of everything you will or will not do. And how long it would take you to do it. Honey, isn't he just amazing?

God knew who my parents would be, and that I would experience abuse, heartbreaks, abandonment, rejection, shame, and plenty of other things. He also knew that out of this pain, a book would be written for other women like me to read. This book would give hope to other women to continue to push through regardless of what you have experienced. Good or bad, God wants to use it for a greater purpose. You think that your pain is all about you? Wrong. Your pain for someone else.

My pain caused me to desire a closer relationship with Christ. I was so desperate for his love, that I was willing to give up someone I felt like I truly loved, and deny my own selfish desires to develop an intimate relationship with my heavenly father. It was one of the best decisions I have made. And girlfriend, I do not plan on going back. There is plenty of work for me to do and plenty of lives for me to touch. Guess what? You too have work to do. Do not allow the pain that you have endured be in vain. Turn your mess into a message. Do not let the lack of love of a father or mother or man keep you from your godly assignment. Or the fact that you may have been abused, misused, talked about, lied on, criticized, molested, raped, had children out of wedlock, keep you down because you can still be used for a purpose greater than you to bring about glory to God.

I need for you to stop here and ask God the question:"Why am I here?" Please sit there for a while and intentionally listen for the answer. Do you already know? Do you think that you are not capable of doing it? Are you afraid? Well, I thought the same thing and look at me now. This is only the beginning.........

"God has a purpose behind every problem."

Chapter 7

What Can You Do?

Is this coming together for you? You should be figuring out who you are, where you come from, and why you are here. It will help you begin to know yourself better and you can begin to love the person that you were created to be (Not who people want you to be. Not who you are pretending to be. You no longer have to pretend.) Once you have embraced the authentic you, you will be unstoppable. Oh, yes you, my sister, will be one fearless and fierce individual. And with that, you now need to understand your own abilities. When God created you with purpose, He also gave you the ability to complete your assignment. Do not think what He has given you is impossible because it isn't. Your past does not dictate, I repeat, it does not dictate your future.

In my journal I wrote that I wanted to go back to school and get my BS in Business Administration before my son graduated. I enrolled at NC Wesleyan College in August of 2014 as a junior. My son was also a junior and my baby girl was a sophomore in high school. They were both very active in sports. As a single mother, I am my children's biggest supporter. I had to get them to and from practice, until my son got his license. I did not miss one game during football or basketball season (home or away) unless they changed the schedule on me. I also volunteered on the athletic council so I could get in the home games free. There were plenty of frustrating days and days of regrets but I was still able to graduate with honors April of 2016, a month before my son graduated from high school.

You have the ability to do whatever you set your mind to do and it be the will of God at the same time. You have to have confidence in yourself and your abilities. Give yourself credit where it is due. God has no limitations, so why do you put a limit on what he can help you do? Come out of the box honey! It is your time to show the world what you can do. We were all given at least one talent and one spiritual gift. Figure out what it is if you don't already know and go to work.

"For it will be like a man going on a journey, who called his servants and entrusted to them his property. To one he gave five talents, to another two, to another one, to each according to his ability. Then he went away". (Matthew 25:14-15) Did you recognize the last few words "according to his ability". You are given gifts and talents but if you do not use them you will lose them. If you are faithful over little, God will give you more. I am still working on believing in myself to do some amazing things. I refuse to be average. Here is a journal entry I made on 4/25/18:

I was once young and restless not fully understanding how bold and beautiful I was, but when I discovered this, it was God that was my guiding light. No matter how hard it gets, no matter if I don't understand the process, no matter if I'm talked about, no matter what comes, my eyes will focus on the Light!!!! Me being average is not acceptable. The fact that I have gotten to know my Source, I am able to live to my fullest potential. Generational curses will be broken. I will not be average anymore and neither will my children or their children. Where does it start? In my mind because I will not be conformed to this world but be transformed by the renewal of my mind. My God is able and and I'm waiting with expectancy! I am and I will be all that He says I will be. In Jesus name. Amen.

You do have the ability to bounce back from any adversity you may have encountered. Let's get away from having pity parties for a long time. Set your mind on the things above as you begin to move in the direction that you were meant to go in anyway. Allow your gifts and talents to make room for you. You have the ability to make a difference in someone else's life according to your own experiences. Most of all, you have the ability to love yourself.

Chapter 8

Where are you Going?

"If you're going through hell, keep going."
Winston Churchill

---

guess by now you see that this process isn't a very easy one. It takes time alone just to figure out who you are. You have identified who you are and where you come from and why you are here. You should know that you have the ability to make a difference in this world through your adversities. Finally, you should know where you are going with all of this.

When reality hit me and the light bulb shone really bright, it was then that I realized that I needed to move. I began to have this hungry for more but not really knowing what the more was. Have you ever felt like that? You wanted to move but you felt stuck? This was not a good feeling for me. I started having doubts because nothing was happening and I found myself laying at the feet of God on a regular basis crying out to him for direction. Honestly, I did not really know what it was that I was expecting. I was starting to love myself and I definitely felt his love, so now what? The what was, I was already doing it standing behind the chair where I participated in adding beauty to people on the outside. Not only that, but encouraging them to go after whatever it was that they wanted (anything from jobs to relationships, which I would be encouraging myself as well).

I can recall having a conversation with one of my clients who was in a very low place in her life. She was having to make a decision that caused her to have thoughts of suicide. The conversation started with me sharing with her how I was learning how to trust God. It was a very tough thing for me to do, because I have always been in control of my life(or so I thought). She began to share with me that she was pregnant but was not sure about keeping the child. She did not want to be anyone's baby mama. She already had a child who was a young teenager and she really didn't see herself starting all over again. That was not the plan for her life. Oh, how God will set you up for those 'godly moments'. Always remember that nothing just happens. If something happens, it was meant to happen- good or bad.

This was the moment that God set aside for me to share the story of how I made a decision concerning my oldest daughter because I did not know how to trust him. She was only fifteen when I got a call from her teacher at school explaining to me that my child was pregnant. "Um, I'm sorry. What did you just say?" I quickly excused myself from doing hair and walked to the back and closed myself in the bathroom. My heart was beating so fast I thought that I was about to have a panic attack. My daughter, fifteen, and expecting a child. Lord, wake me up right now and tell me it is only a dream, I thought to myself. The teacher repeated that my daughter was pregnant and afraid to tell me. I spoke briefly to my daughter and with everything in me I held back the tears of disappointment. "We will talk when I get home." I returned back to work barely able to talk to my client.

When I arrived home later that day, my daughter and I had a conversation about whether or not she was ready to be a mother. I explained to her how I would have to be responsible for both of them, including her brother and sister, because she was still a child herself. I was in school working on my associates degree, working full time, and a full time single mother of three. How in the world was I going to do this? My daughter suggested an abortion and I agreed with no hesitation. I actually was glad she said it first, because I was thinking it anyway. A week after her sixteenth birthday, I took her to have the procedure done. She and I did not have the best relationship then and after her abortion, it only seemed to make it worse. I was not proud of the decision, but during my process, I realized that I had trust issues. I used this story to encourage my client to just *try* Jesus. I suggested that she not make her decision based on her emotions. God will supply her every need if she just trusts him. He is not man that he shall lie or repent. He has to keep his every word. I am happy to say that she kept her child and is so happy that she did. He has brought so much joy in her life. Also, my daughter is expecting a daughter of her own in a few weeks. God is a God of many chances and I am so glad that he saw fit to give me a chance to share to others in hopes of giving them hope in their own situations.

It is now clear to me where I am going. I am going higher and higher in Christ as he is teaching me to love him, myself, and others. My destination here on earth is to reach other hurting women and encourage them as they begin their own process with learning how to love themselves, God, and others. I must complete the work that he has assigned specifically to me, so when I get to heaven I can hear him say "well done my good and faithful servant".

Where are you going? Where do you see yourself in the next month, year or two? Yes, you want to be loved. You want to experience a real godly healthy relationship. Me too. But you and I have to be processed so that we can appreciate the love that will be given to us and the love we will be able to give away. Loving others in such a way that we are okay with not receiving it in return because we know who loves us the most. Everything God created you to do, you have the ability to do it -big or small. Allow God to be the author and finisher of your faith. Do not allow your current or past circumstances to dictate your future destination. You have work to do while you are being processed. Remember that you can be used right where you are now.

"Your present situation is not your final destination"
Richard_quotes

Chapter 9

Own Your Truth

"You can't go back and change the beginning but you can start where you are and change the ending"
C.S. Lewis

---

ou have discovered who you are, where you are from, you acknowledge that you have purpose, and that you also have the ability to fulfill that purpose. You're now heading in the right direction. You have accepted what you have discovered and now I need you to gather all of that together and own your truth. God created you for a reason. No matter what you went through you can still be used. I had to learn to own my truth no matter how it looked or how it made me feel. I had to own the fact that this is my story. Period. I come from an imperfect family and I'm sure there are families out here worse than mine. There are other women who have had worse experiences than I have had. It doesn't matter to me if the story is worse or if the story is better, what matters is that I have accepted my truth.

This process was difficult as well. I did not know where to start, so guess what I did? I asked for help. I found a mentor to help me figure it out. I told you before that I started having this hunger on the inside of me that was desiring to do more. My mentor told me that she understood where I was because she too have experienced that feeling. She warned me that she was going to stay on me and I assured her that was exactly what I needed. My first assignment was to do a ten minute video. I could talk about anything from childhood to the present. I made the video. As I was creating the video, I started remembering things about my childhood and started realizing that some of these things I had suppressed. I was actually angry at myself, my mother, and my father.

The anger I had towards my mother was because she left me at such a young age, even though it was not her choice. Or was it? I have been told that we actually can shorten our days on this earth based on how we live. If you live a fast life, you have a chance at dying fast. I was only ten for goodness sake! The very first death experience and it was my mother. Not only that, but I had a father who was very inconsistent in my life. He was only two and a half hours away and rarely came to see me. He was busy raising someone else's children. I know that sounds mean. I get it. He married a woman with three children, so he had to take on the responsibility of the children as well. Trust me when I say, I get it. What I do not get is that he would neglect his own biological child. There would be times where I would pack my clothes and be waiting on him to come get me and he wouldn't show up. And he did not call me either.

Have you ever been let down by your parents, or someone that you really cared about? Have you been told something and it's a lie? Did you try to make up excuses for them only because you didn't want to face the truth? (wiping my tears as I speak) I do not have the answers to why it happened like this, but I do know that it happened. That was my father and I still had love for him no matter how many times he lied to me. That was my daddy y'all. The good, the bad, and the imperfect father.

It is sad to say that most of my memories of my mother were not the best. Me and my siblings were left home alone most of the time. There were times when we did not have much to eat, and go days without electricity. You remember the welfare cheese, butter, and rice? Honey, yes. I was eating rice probably every day back then. Funny thing though as much as I ate it back then, I still like rice and butter. I also remember powdered milk we would have with the cereal (Oh the memories). When my mother was home she was either in the bed or entertaining company. Oh and I will never forget, we had to clean up after these grown people when the party was over (tip please!). This was my mother. The good, the bad and the imperfect, and I still had love for her. She was *my* mother. Do you get the point here? You have to own your truth. Only you know what you have endured. Only you can tell it the way you need to tell it. No one else can walk in your shoes. And believe me, some people will probably choose to wear their own shoes once they take a look at yours.

I have had some dark days in my life. As a young teenager I tried to commit suicide after my first heartbreak. This was my first year in highschool and I was dating a senior. I thought I was doing something. Of course he was older and more experienced, so once he got tired of me and wanted to move on to the next, he dumped me. Sad, but true. I really did not know how to handle that. I was already sick with a cold and decided to drink the whole bottle of prescription cold medicine. I had to be rushed to the hospital and have my stomach pumped. All because I wanted to be loved and they did not want to love me anymore.

Luckily, that young girl in me bounced on after that and have had plenty more heartbreaks. I may have even broken some myself. You see even when you do not fully understand where you are going in life, God has a way of looking out for us. How faithful he is to you when you are not faithful to him? You have to just learn how to admit when you do not know any better and learn how to do better. It is your story, your life, your future. Just own it already!!!!

Chapter 10

Forgiveness is a Must!

"Life becomes easier when you learn to accept an apology you never got"

Robert Brault

orking on yourself can be challenging, especially if you believe that nothing is wrong with you. You must learn how to develop yourself into the best version of you. You are now learning to own your truth, learning to affirm yourself, learning to journal through your process, and now it is time to forgive yourself, and ask God to forgive you for all the bad decisions that you made that caused your heartache or someone else heartache. Also forgive those who have done hurtful things to you. Yes ma'am, once you have asked God for forgiveness, you have to forgive yourself also, so that you can begin to forgive others. You are part of the problem, and Hallelujah you can also be a part of the solution. You can no longer use the blame game as if you are totally innocent. Nor can you have self pity parties either, as if you are a victim. If you are jamming to your own pity, it stops right now. I want you to keep an open mind and put away your emotions for just a few minutes. We will come back and acknowledge them shortly, but right now I need for you to continue to own your truth as you forgive yourself for those relationships that you knew were not any good from the start, but you stayed in it. You saw the red flags before you even allowed yourself to get involved with him, but you did anyway.

The abusive relationship that I was in, I saw plenty of red flags and I continued in the relationship. I now realize that it had a lot to do with that desire of wanting to be loved and not receiving love from my mother or father. Therefore, I would accept anything just to say I had a man. The fact that I did not have enough courage to leave this relationship after all the fighting and cheating, I had to acknowledge that I made the decision to stay regardless of why I stayed, I still stayed. I stayed with him after being choked and thrown from the bed, catching him at the hotel with another woman, and after I almost killed him and could have went to prison. None of this was love. There was an unhealthy soul tie between us. About five years after our final breakup, we met for lunch. I explained to him that I needed to forgive him so that I could move on with my life. Holding the next man accountable for the things that he did to me was just not the business. I felt pretty good after the conversation and was ready to move forward, or so I thought. The problem here is that I continued to get in relationships with my mess. Mess that

I really needed to deal with before allowing myself to enter into another relationship. "Friend zone" is as far as I got.

Is this what you desire for yourself? I hope you said no. You deserve better and you do not need to be placed in a "friend zone" with marriage benefits. Stop cooking for him, cleaning his house, washing his clothes, and expecting him to change. Not!! But since you have done these things and put your valuable time into it, just admit to it and tell yourself that you are sorry for allowing yourself to be in that situation and that you deserve better, but just did not know better. Now that you know better you will definitely do better.

While Trooper was overseas and I was being 'processed', I had to forgive myself for willingly staying in the "friend zone" after being told that he was not ready for commitment. In this creative mind of mine, I had created this fairytale of us being together and he would change his mind about us. I volunteered to remodel his sunroom (with his money of course. I was not that crazy) even after the fact, I accidently ran into another female he was dealing with, at his house. She was there looking to have some landscaping done. I still put my hard sweat and time into it too, but it did not change the fact that he was just not interested in having a committed relationship with me. My fairytale was just a fairytale and I had to accept it and move on. I forgave myself for that. I accepted my false readings, cried my eyes out, and forcefully moved on.

This is really embarrassing. It is my truth though. I have accepted it and working on moving forward by forgiving this foolishness and forgiving him for lying to me. At the end of the day the forgiveness part is really for you, not them. It will give you a peace and great joy on the inside. When you acknowledge that you messed up and refuse to stay in your mess. Guess what? You already won. You are looking at a brighter future for yourself.

Listen, I had to write my mother and father a letter and tell them that I forgive them. I forgave them for abandoning me, rejecting me, lying to me, and not truly loving me. The only thing that really helped me with this part is accepting that they just did not know better.

So are you open to forgiving those who have done you wrong? Even if they do not ask for forgiveness? Remember, it is for you. You are being processed to learn how to love and in order to love, you must first learn how to forgive. It is definitely not that easy but you can do it. Write down in your journal the ones that you need to forgive. It does not necessarily have to be a male relationship. It could be a family member, church member, girl friend, and maybe even a co-worker. Whomever it may be, you are fully capable of forgiving them.

I did not forget about your feelings. I told you that we would come back and acknowledge them. You are allowed to feel how you feel but you cannot allow those feelings to dictate your decisions. Most females tend to let their feelings control their actions. My advice to you from now on, recognize your feelings and ask yourself why are you feeling that way? Is it really about the current situation or something from the past? Allow yourself fifteen minutes before you respond. By this time you should be calmed down. Now, if you are feeling the same way after taking some time to think about it, you should be calm enough to respond properly. Learn to forgive quickly because life is too short. Do not get caught by God with unforgiveness in your heart. Let's pray:

Father, thank you for forgiving this beautiful lady when she is out of order. I appreciate the fact that once she repents, you do not throw that sin back in her face. Please help her to demonstrate that same kind of forgiveness towards herself and others. Now, that she is learning how to love, she understands that keeping a record of wrongdoing is not love. Help her not to keep record and to trust you helping her to do it. Thank you again for forgiving her and teaching her how to forgive.

In Jesus name, Amen

"If we really want to love, we must learn how to forgive."
Mother Teresa (Humanitarian)

Chapter 11

I am who I say I am

Today I choose to live with gratitude for the love that feels my heart the peace that passes understanding and the whisper of hope that reminds me with God all things are possible counting my blessings

---

I finally came to grips with all the pain I had been avoiding and suppressing for so long. Moving on to the next relationship and taking all my baggage had become the norm for me. The desire to be loved seemed to be impossible. I did not believe that it was even possible for me. What is wrong with me? The first thing that came to mind is that I was not worthy of being loved. I had failed at it so many times; however, I was willing to learn how and I started by owning my truth, and by learning how to affirm myself.

Have you ever seen the television show *Being Mary Jane?* Mary Jane was a beautiful successful news anchor who desired to be married and have children one day. She seemed to be the only one of her siblings that was doing well financially. The family had a high level of dependency on her. So between her trying to help out with family issues, working towards a job promotion, and wanting to get married, she was emotionally out of whack. I do believe however that Mary Jane desired to be a better her, regardless of the many things that were going on around her, so she would write words of affirmation on her walls, mirrors, and even on the headboard of her bed to remind herself to stay focused and positive. The question with that though, is did she believe what she was affirming from these quotes and other affirmation of words?

If you have experienced some level of abuse, whether physical, emotional, or verbal, did you find the verbal abuse to be the most difficult to heal from? In what ways have you tried to recondition your thought process? Do you have memories of being told that you were nothing, no one will ever want you because you have children, you're sorry, you are a bitch, Well, I have been told all the above and probably some more negative things that had some great effect on my self-esteem in the past. I needed to control my thoughts and retrain my mind set. In my opinion, verbal abuse is worse than physical abuse. Bruises go away in time, but words remain as if they were glued to your brain. It does not take much to trigger those negative thoughts. This is the main reason you must learn to affirm yourself on a consistent basis.

Affirmations are positive words that you should intentionally tell yourself daily. Did you know that the words you speak have power? Positive or negative. You can choose which one you want to guide your life; however I highly recommend that you choose to speak positive things. The more that you speak positive things, the more positive things will begin to happen. "Death and life are in the power of the tongue and those who love it will eat its fruit" (Proverbs 18:21 ESV) You should want to see positive things happen in your life. Even though some bad things cannot be avoided; you can learn to respond to it in a healthy way.

Let's go back again to when I first surrendered. I had to learn how to pray, so I wrote down scriptures and put them on index cards. I placed the cards on a small poster board in my bathroom. Listen, *my bathroom became a War Room* . I placed words of affirmation on my mirror that says: 1) I am the daughter of a King 2) My faith is not my feelings but the Word of God and 3) I am fearfully and wonderfully made in God's image. When I would go into the bathroom, faithfully I would see the scriptures and affirmations. Two of my favorite scriptures in particular is Jeremiah 29:11, which reminded me daily that God had a plan and a purpose for my life. James 1:2 reminded me to count it all joy when I fall into various trials, because the testing of my faith would produce steadfastness. It is during your tribulations when your faith is being tested. Don't get upset with what you go through because it's only used to strengthen you and make you draw closer to God. You must remember that no matter what you go through, God is still in control.

On May 30, 2018, I noted some affirmations to remind myself I was: forgiven, enough, beautiful, wealthy, powerful, loved by God, special, a business owner, healthy, faithful, purposed, faithful, bold, courageous, an author, and a speaker/coach. I want you to do the same thing when you start to think negative, I need for you to begin speaking positive words to yourself. Write them down and place them somewhere you know that you will see them all the time. Tell yourself that you are beautiful. Tell yourself that you are more than a conqueror. Tell yourself that you can and you will succeed. Tell yourself that all things are possible through Christ if you believe. You have to trust him.

When you speak the positive affirmations aloud, you must believe it. You have to be consistent with it every day, no exceptions! I would listen to different motivational videos on Youtube while I was working out. This would help me to stay focused and keep a positive attitude throughout the day. I mentioned to you earlier that being an encourager was my spiritual gift, but during my process it was not always easy to keep myself encouraged.

One of my prayers is to be married to a good godly man. I have been single for twelve years and my heart truly desires to be married. I know that marriage can be challenging and rewarding. When God decides to release my husband for us to meet, I need to already be in a good space of loving who I am. I need to be able to be happy even if my husband isn't. I need to know that my identity is not in a man. I will be complete in God, so that I will be capable of making deposits to my relationship instead of withdrawals. I honestly believe that God is going to blow my mind. He is able to do exceeding abundantly above all that I can ask or think. I will continue to affirm myself on a daily basis and

I highly recommend that you do the same. Begin to say it to the point of believing it no matter what happens.

Speak over your own life. Encourage yourself. It starts with you owning your truth and then affirming who you really are. You are no longer afraid or ashamed. Can you see yourself being bolder and having more confidence? Nobody can take it from you because they did not give it to you anyway. God gave it to you. They can't take your power unless you give it to them. Now, go and get your index cards and begin to write down your affirmations and place them everywhere you can see them on a daily basis. Remember, do not only say it, but believe it!

Chapter 12

Journal Your Way Through

What a comfort is this journal. I tell myself to myself and throw the burden on my book and feel relieved.

Anne Lister

---

mentioned to you earlier that I started journaling at a young age. I would journal consistently for a while and then I would stop, but it has been a great way of helping me to release the thoughts in my mind or the pain that I felt. I was not always able to express my feelings without the fear of being judged, or being told how I should feel. I have continued to write things down that I wanted to see God do for me and the people in my life. I was writing and believing in what I was hoping would happen. During my process, I was definitely doing a lot of journaling. Remember when I shared with you that I was trying to learn how to trust God? This was during the time that my youngest daughter was having to choose a college. I have decided to share some of my journal entries during my process. This is a judge free zone here. Everything that you are about to read is real and written exactly how I wrote it. No editing.

5/15/17: Oh Lord how excellent is thou name. I thank you for waking me up this morning. I can say thank you, thank you, thank you, for loving me and being patient with me. Even in those moments I want to be in control. All things work for the good of those who love you and are called unto your purpose. I let my emotions get the best of me at times. I am still in progress on that. The fact that I was created to be emotional but yet I can't let my emotions dictate my faith can be very challenging. Yet you are strong for me in my time of weakness. Yesterday was Mother's Day and I truly enjoyed my kids. We all went to church, they cook dinner and we did a photo shoot for KyNazi's T-shirt line. We all just laughed and loved on each other all day. Thank you for that. Thank you that Kerra is noticing her growth. Help her to continue to strive daily to become the woman that you predestined her to be. Help her to prioritize when it comes to her money and her time. Thank you for the offer that TeeTee got at UMO. I am overjoyed. I see that you do answer prayers and I just have to continue to believe that what I am asking for particularly for myself also come in due time. I know that you will continue to keep my daughter as she goes off to school and she will excel even more with your help. Thank you!! Feeling happy In Jesus name Amen

5/ 27/17: Father yesterday ended in a very hard day. Mind was going everywhere. Drinking and nothing felt better. Crying and praying but nothing makes sense. Asking for peace in my situation. The pain is severe. The thought was to give up. Why so much pain?

What is the purpose behind this pain? Why do I feel stuck? What was the reminder of Hebrews 10:23? Where is my husband? What more can I do in my waiting season to keep from growing weary? Why does sin seems to look better next to righteousness? How do you encourage when you need encouraging? How long? How long? How long? Lay your burden before God and he will give you rest. I really need rest. What is it that you want me to learn from all this? To trust? I'm not doing a good job. Whatever you are doing in my life I need help to endure the pain. Somehow it will make me a better person. There is a purpose in this pain but I have a hard time with it. Help me to trust not only for others but for myself. Help me to recall your word and believe in it with all my heart. There is a purpose and plan for my life.(underline plan and purpose) Help me not to miss it. I need you more and more each day to do your will and not mine. I asked you again if either if the trooper is not the man that you are preparing for me please remove any feelings that I have for him. Give me total peace. No bitterness or sadness but absolutely joy. Because if he isn't the one Father I know he will still be just as good as the trooper. I'm ready to be released because my heart is attached along with my mind and I need your help to get me through. And if he is help me to continue on my journey fully trusting this process and not wavering. Help me to believe Hebrews 10:23! Renew my strength Restore my joy and Increase my faith

In Jesus name Amen

Waiting on you Father

6/ 24/18: Lord I have made it to Myrtle Beach to spend the next four nights here. It is a well needed break. During this break I am hoping for clarity. I want you to help me write exactly what needs to be written for the book "Processed for the Promise discovering your worth" No longer will I be afraid of opening up to new relationships. I will be bold and confident. Thank you for equipping me to do what you will have me to do. Lives will change and I will change for the better. Thank you for the community of good people who all desire to become better. Light my fire again Lord and help me stay lit. Help me not think or say anything negative toward anyone else. I look forward to going to the next retreat. My time is my time and I will celebrate others while I wait. I am excited for my G sisters as they all as have encountered your Holy Spirit today. May we all continue to be fierce and fearless.

In Jesus name Amen

10/2/18: Lord you are so good to me! I love you and thank you for loving me. I was able to attend BOSC which cost $899 and I was still able to eat and pay bills. Now I want to do Jasmine's Boot Camp which cost $799 and I am expecting again not to lack. I will be able to attend my son's homecoming and go to Grindfest. I asked that my son's student loans be paid off, my student loan paid off in full, and Teliyah graduating debt-free and it will happen. I will write this book with your help. You will give me exactly what I need in order to make this book a bestseller. All things are possible. My children and grandchildren must know that we have greatness on the inside of us and we must leave this world with our legacy behind. I am absolutely nervous but I am confident that once I write this book and it does really well my faith will increase. During the women's *retreat I look forward to you speaking to my heart and guiding me exactly where I need to go. Help me to activate the power that lives within me. You are inside of me and you created me therefore I am able to do all that you planned for me. Please comfort Taj's family as well as Hiquekka's family. They will be truly missed. You know what is best. We just have to continue to trust your way and not our own. Great is your faithfulness! Thank you for confirmations for my book, my husband, my children, and help me continue to walk in boldness and confidence. Help me not to be easily offended. I remember to stay focused on you and your word. I thank you and give you the praise! I am expecting good things to happen to and for me I'm expecting the aha moments. In Jesus name Amen*

Dated 11/19/18

Lord I will continue to give you praise this book will be completed obstacles are coming but you are still greater. With children, car, health you have it all in control. I trust you father!

In Jesus name

Amen

You see how if you write it down and believe, that God will make things happen? Do you have a journal? If not, I encourage you to go and purchase you one and make it your process journal. You are being processed for that Real Love, that husband, that child, that promotion, that ministry, that book, and so much more. You must understand that God has to make sure that we are ready for what He is about to do in your life. Keep a record of it all, so you can look back and see that he remained faithful to you. Write the vision and believe.

You are really making progress here my sister. Don't stop reading now, you have just a few more things to consider while you are being processed for real love. It is time to surround yourself around positive people. I will meet you over there in that positive environment. Hurry up!

Chapter 13

Positive Vibes Only!

"Surround yourself with people that reflect who do you want to be and how you want to feel energies are contagious"
Rachel Wochin

---

ou are making real progress here. I am super proud of you. You have owned your truth. You are affirming yourself. You are journaling your process and you are learning to forgive yourself and others. Working on you, which is the best thing that you can do, involves a lot of intentional decisions. One of those decisions should be for you to surround yourself around positive, motivated, dreamers who know how to execute. There is a saying that people come into your life for a reason, a season, and a lifetime. Everybody is not meant to stay in your life forever. The ones that come in for a short period of time is purposed just for that time. They come to serve a purpose and there is a lesson to be learned. What you need to do is learn to recognize the lesson, receive it, and move forward. Look back over some of your not so good relationships. Do you realize that you made it through those relationships? You may not have understood why the relationship may have ended, but you did survive it.

Let's go back to the abusive relationship. When God was dealing with me during my surrendering process, he showed me that this was generational, I was stronger than I thought, and I was also weak in some areas.

What I finally realized is that I didn't want to keep on having meaningless relationships. I am blessed to have some really good girl friends that have been in my life since middle school. But after discovering that I have purpose, I also discovered that it would take other people to help me get where I needed to be. It was now time for me to be intentional about allowing new relationships to enter into my life. I had a strong desire to become better than what I was already. With that being said, I prayed to God to surround me with the right people who could help me to get where I needed to be. This meant I would need to surround myself around positive people who desired to excel at life from the inside out.

When you work on yourself from the inside out, you will become stronger in your faith, family, fitness, and your finances. Those are the main core areas of your life. Allow yourself to be around people with positive vibes *only* and who also desire to be strengthen in those same core areas. You want the kind of people who are going to push you to become better, hold you accountable for what you say that you want, and not be afraid to call you out on your mess.

God is very intentional about everything that he does in your life; therefore you should be just as intentional , especially with what you ask for in prayer. I told you that I did ask him to place the right people in my life that would help me to get to where I needed to go and he did just that. I knew that I had purpose now, and my heart was very excited about doing something that God would be pleased with.

God's ways and thoughts are so much more greater than ours. Let me tell you just how amazing and humorous he can be. I asked for the right people to come into my life and he sent me a whole community of women and men. Did you just hear what I said? Not one or two or ten people, but an entire community! The funny part is that I said that I do not care to "do" women like that. They are just drama and I can do without that in my life. The community consist of men and women from the west coast to the east coast. Yes, with different time zones and all, but we still communicated on a daily basis.

January of 2018, is the first time that I was introduced to Kendell Ficklin. He is the CEO of Grindation, which consist of group coaching sessions, community group discussions, access to live Q&A, and other tools and resources that will help you to transform your life. Kendall and I spoke briefly over the phone about me wanting to open my own hair salon but I was afraid. He said just do it. He suggested that I apply for a business loan and stop being afraid. And I'm thinking, really? Just like that? After talking to Kendell, I was still scared to move for some reason.

I have been doing hair for twenty years and I also have a BS in Business Administration, yet I was still afraid to move. Later in March, Kendell came to a hotel in Rocky Mount, North Carolina to speak and I made sure I was going to be there to meet him in person. I was so sure about going that I left my client under the dryer (do not judge me). Luckily, the hotel was only about five minutes from the shop and my coworker was nice enough to look after my client when I left.

I was truly amazed at how confident this short guy, maybe about 5'5 tall, bald head with light brown eyes entered into the room and spoke with such power. It was about ten women in the room, some of whom already had the pleasure of meeting him, and they all seemed to be excited about the event. I can remember him telling us it was time to let go. Let go of the guy or the relationship that was no good for us, let go of past hurts, stop making excuses, and get our power back. He explained that women had more power than we thought we did, but we keep giving it away to the wrong somebody. He then goes on to explain what a Proverbs 31 woman was. She was a woman who got up early to prepare food for her family, she was an entrepreneur, who made her own clothes, she knew how to store up for hard times, and her children called her blessed.

I do not know about you, but I am striving to be a Proverbs 31 woman. I do desire to be married and have a healthy marriage, regardless of the abuse I may have experienced. And to listen to a man say out loud that you and I both have all this power, but we keep freely giving it away to people who do not deserve it and then we sit in our pity and complain instead of doing something about it. We need to take a look at ourselves and do an assessment. What does it take to make you better? Before Kendell left, I signed up to be a part of Grindation, where I also became a GWoman.

GWomen would meet everyday on Zoom for a 30 minutes motivational call. Do you see how God is able to do far greater than what you expect? God sent me a whole community of women that came from all different states, different backgrounds, different looks, but one thing that we all had in common is that we were all striving to become better. And we were all willing to help each other. Never in a million years would I have thought that God would have put me with a bunch of women. I'm sure you probably think like I once did, about some women. The fact that some of them can be full of drama and "catty" I also understand now that it is a deeper than the surface of things. There is a strong root to why we act the way we do.

Have you ever experienced situations where you were hanging out with people who were just negative all the time? All they seem to do is complain but was not trying to do anything to change their situation, and they would suck up all your energy just from you listening to them. Start being very intentional about who you allow to enter into your space. Whether you are related to them, dating them, or just friends. The people in your life should be adding to you, not constantly taking away. Do not feel bad if it is a friend who has been there for quite some time. Some seasons last longer than others. Just learn from the friendship and keep moving.

I am so grateful to have prayed that prayer. I was able to meet my GSisters and GBrothers all at Grindfest just a couple of weeks ago. My sisters are setting good examples, encouraging me, and steadily pouring back into my life. I am also now surrounded around some positive men who also strive to be better. That includes with other men, their spouses (if they have one), and their family. They have set the standards of what a I should consider in a man when my time comes. I can hear the chants now "GMen!" "We Lit!" "Boogame!". Whomever you decide to allow to be in your space is completely up to you, but I do advise that you choose wisely.

Chapter 14

It's A Heart Thing

Believe in what you're praying for. If God has placed that desire on your heart, then you must fear not, for He is with you.

At the age of 30, I discovered that I had never been in love. I had been lusting in all my "relationships" or "friendships". After my ex-husband, all other relationships never seem to be able to go further than the friends with benefits zone. No one wanted the title, and I really wasn't ready, although I thought I was. There was a lot of work that needed to be done on the inside of me. The outside appearance did a great job with covering up all the anger, rejection, self-doubt, fear, insecurities, abandonment, and depression that I was really battling with. I was never given a real sex talk, nor was I ever told how beautiful I was and that I was worth waiting for. But my heart still desired to love and be loved.

Does this sound familiar to you? You deserve better than that. No one may have told you that you are worthy and that you are enough, but you are. If your heart desires to be married then it's time to start thinking and acting like a wife. You do not have to be in the friend zone forever when you know that you are wife material. The men only do as much as you allow them to do. Set your standards and stand strong with what you want. Some qualities that should be a must is that they have a job, car, and a house. The number one should be that he loves God and puts him first. If they do not have that, in my opinion, it would be a deal breaker.

There was a young intelligent dark smooth skinned guy with pretty white teeth (Yes, I am a fool for nice white teeth) that was also in my life during the time I was seeing the trooper. He was definitely the ideal guy for me, but the fact that we had different beliefs kept us at the friendship level. We would have great conversations, hours at a time, and we hung out on a regular basis. He would open up the car door for me, even if I drove. I often asked God about him but he wasn't the one. We had a season together where we both were growing. I saw changes in him since the day we met. We actually had a great friendship for two years and then he met someone. This of course, change the trajectory of our relationship, which I knew would happen. I was honestly excited for him, but upset with God because I was still waiting.

You do not have to pout when someone else reaches that place that you so wish to be. Your timing is not their timing. You must just continue to believe that it will happen for you. Keep being obedient and being prayerful. Make sure that you are being specific in what you desire in a husband. Do not settle. Keep in mind that you have made some changes in your life and going back to those old ways should *not* be an option for you. Stay focused. Continue to delight yourself in the Lord, and he will give you the desires of your heart. When you find yourself sitting and thinking why hasn't anything happened for you yet? Start reflecting over your life, and concentrate on the things that are happening for you. In your waiting season you must be able to have patience.

After the Holy Spirit spoke to me, while I was lying helpless on the floor, telling me that I had a second chance, I was overjoyed and anxious about when the second chance would happen. I had actually tried to figure out how he was going to do it too. This was not a good idea, especially because there was a time period when nothing seem to be happening at all for me. Yes, I desired to do this God's way this time, but honey I had a few pity parties. You know the kind of party where you turn on your bluetooth speaker, play Pandora, pour you a few glasses of wine or a mixed drink, and just whine about everything. You may need this, but I recommend that you do not stay at the party long. One day is enough, then you need to put your big girl panties on, dry your tears, and start moving again.

The closer you get to your breakthrough, the tougher things seem to become. Do not give in. It is only a test. During your test is when it seems that God is far away, but he is not. He may be silent because you are testing, but he has not left your side. Pray that your heart desires fall in line with the desires that God has for you. The goal is to do the things that he wants you to do. It is my belief that if you desire something that he will give it to you. It may not be how you thought it would be but just the way he needed it to be. Just trust him.

Chapter 15

Content In This Season

> "To be content doesn't mean you don't desire more, it means you're thankful for what you have and patient for what's to come".
>
> Tony Gaskins

Are you happy and content in your current situation? Your heart is desiring some things and now you have to wait for the promise to manifest. How are you waiting? When I began this process I was doing a lot of crying and pouting. My thoughts were only on what God had told me. The problem with this is that he never gave me a specific time or date. He did reassure me that I would get a second chance at love, his way. I can understand why God does not show us everything before he gives it to us because we probably would choose not to go through the process.

November 2016, I attended an event called *The Altar Call Experience*. It had been a full year since I had been abstinent and

I was having a hard time with the trooper being back home and we were not communicating like I had imagined we would. I was constantly asking God was I in the right place. At this event, that I made myself go to, I asked God to show up for me. I went with expectations that he would answer my prayer. It seemed as if every other month I was ready to throw in the towel and go back to my old ways. Of course, you know that that would be the worse decision to make. I was really having a hard time being content in my season.

Kim Hodges, who was the speaker of the night, demonstrated how we go to the altar and ask God to do all these things for us, but as soon as we leave the altar, we have picked that problem right back up. Why do you do this? It is possible that you have control issues. You say you want God to do a thing for you, but when God does not move fast enough, you pick your stuff up and try to handle it yourself. How did that turn out? That same baggages that you keep carrying around seem to have both of your hands full. You have the luggage with wheels in one hand, a large tote bag, a pocketbook, a bookbag, and a book to read in the other hand. You are so loaded down that you cannot receive the blessings that God has for you. Your hands are too full to receive anything else.

The Holy Spirit was in that place. Women were crying out to God with their faces to the floor in worship. Some were walking around worshipping and speaking in tongues. I was over in a corner to myself just asking him to show up for me because I could feel his presence. While I was worshipping, a woman walked over to me and she said, "The spirit is telling me that you are going to be a beautiful bride, and your husband is going to be a mighty man of God. I feel that you already know him too." She then asked me," Do you have a daughter?" I told her," Yes, I have two". She said," Well, your daughter is proud of you". Not sure which daughter she was talking about, but all I could do was cry and tell God thank you over and over again. He had showed up like I expected and I was not disappointed; however, I started to get anxious and impatient about what the Holy Spirit said.

Can you recall a time when your mom or dad may have promised you something but did not quite give you an exact time when you would get what they promised? Were you constantly reminding them what they told you? And they would tell you to wait. Huh? Wait? Yes, you will get what God has promised but you may have to wait. While you are waiting you must learn to be content. This was very challenging for me at first. All I know is that the Holy Spirit spoke and I was ready to receive, but it was not going to happen like that. I had started to make being married an idol. I discussed with you earlier in the book about how the Israelites were worshipping an idol, and God was jealous.The same applies here. Anything that we focus on more than we do God is an idol. I honestly did not realize this until I heard a sermon on idolatry. I was so ashamed, but I repented and asked God to help me be content until it was my time. I had to learn how to focus on other things, one being my purpose.

Being single and living wholeheartedly for Christ is not easy at all. You must learn to be content though. Enjoy being single.

You do not have to share the time you spend with God with anyone else. Once you begin dating with a purpose, you will have to share that time with your man. There are some advantages to being single and you should enjoy every minute of it. Start taking yourself on dates, go have a dinner and movie, take about 15 minutes out your day and spend alone, and go on trips without having to check in with anybody. There is peace. Being married, you can still do some of these things as long as your husband still get what he needs. Let's pause here and pray:

Father, thank you for loving this beautiful woman. Her heart desires to love and be loved. She is trusting you for the moment when you will place the right godly man in her life. But while she is waiting Lord, I ask that you help her to be happy and content in her singleness. Give her the wisdom and self control that she needs. We are forever grateful for all that you do.

In Jesus name,

Amen

Chapter 16

♥♥

Where is the Love?

Self-love is not selfish; you cannot truly love another until you know how to love yourself.

Learning how to love yourself can be very challenging. First of all, you have to be willing to admit that you have a problem with fully loving yourself. You're thinking, I do love me. Do you really? What are you doing that proves and shows that? Earlier, I mentioned how important it was to affirm yourself. Well, affirming you is not the hard part, believing it is. I honestly thought that I loved myself, but I really did not know how to love myself. I would allow myself to be in certain situations that were not healthy at all. I had the outer appearance looking good but on the inside I was 'tore up from the floor up'. Walking into a room full of beautiful women would cause me to shrink my own thoughts of me being just as beautiful. Have you ever allowed yourself to be used because you did not know your worth? I am guilty of that. I was afraid that if I say no to him, he wouldn't want me. If I missed his call he will be upset or if I take half the day to respond to his text message he would probably ignore me. All kinds of thoughts would go through my mind. I did not know for sure if it would happen but because I did not love myself or know my worth I did not want to take any chances.

Oh, but when you come into the right relationship, things begin to change. You must ask God to show you how to see yourself as he sees you. You do know that he truly adores you no matter what. There is nothing that you can do to change that. This is why he absolutely need to be a major part of your life. There is no man on earth who can meet his standards, but it's important that they try to model it. Our problem is that we will love in the condition that….That you are being nice to me, you are having a good day, you are giving me everything I want, or you are not getting on my last nerve. That is not love at all.

I absolutely tried my hardest to get Trooper to love me. Nothing that I did seem to impress him at all. While he was overseas, I remodeled his sunroom (he paid for it and I did the work) washed old laundry that had been there since he had left, cleaned the entire house after his mom had new carpet put in, and not once did I mention all the women's items that I found while cleaning up. When he returned home, he took two weeks to see me and did not show any appreciation for what I had done. Apparently, he was moving on but not with me. I was completely heartbroken.

Here is where I had to accept things as they were. I was no longer going to force anyone to love me. When you love someone, you have to be able to love them without any expectations of them loving you back. You have to just do your part. I know that I have the capacity to love, but I also want to be loved too. In 1 Corinthians 13:4-7, Paul is telling the church of Corinth how the church is to love one another. It says: "Love is patient and kind; love does not envy or boast; it is not arrogant or rude. It does not insist on its own way; it is not irritable or resentful; it does not rejoice at wrongdoing, but rejoices in the truth. Love bears all things, believes all things, hopes all things, endure all things". Can you love like this? Can you honestly say that you are loving people at the level in which God intends for us to love? You are loving them with no expectations and doing it unconditionally. That agape love, the kind of love that has the power to move you to meet someone's need with no expectations in return. No. I cannot say that. I was expecting the trooper to be with me and love me as I deserved to be loved. I can say this though, I am striving and willing to love like this but it will take Christ to help me. This is not easy. Just today in bible study, my pastor reminded us that, you and I are both waiting on the other person to love, instead of just doing our part. You may not get the love that you want right away, but this is why love is patient.

That's one of many reasons why God is so amazing. He has patience. He waited on me and you. He knew that I would soon turn to the Man who could love me like no one else could. He did not judge me, did not remind me of my wrongdoings, nor did he get irritated waiting. Just think about that for a minute. Would you not want someone to love you like this? Especially since your mess is raggedy and your stuff does stink. I am imperfect that has someone perfect to love and to love me back. Mmmmm that is good to me!

The way that God describes love means that you and I will have to love those who have mistreated us, those who we do not think deserve it, and those who do not love us back. I find myself thinking that maybe this is one of the reasons that I was not able to have a healthy relationship. I was not able to love myself this way, nor was I loving on God. All I wanted was to love this man.

Chapter 17

Girl, Walk in Your Purpose

"Our lives have a purpose and a meaning. Our very existence is not an accident of procreation neither did we come to the earth to simply exist."

Pastor Yemisi Ashimolowo

You ever had the feeling of not being able to breathe? It felt as if a sudden brisk of heat filled your body and the palms of your hands are hot and sweaty. You are beginning to feel anxious and quickly you gasp for air. Just breathe. Inhale. Exhale. One more time.

I was having a panic attack. This wasn't the first time but it surely had been years since I had this experience. Not a good feeling at all. The thought of Trooper being with someone else had my throat closing in and my heart racing like Dale Earnhardt on the race track. "Help me Lord!" Daily I had to seek his face because I could not understand why this soul tie was causing me so much pain. A pain that seemed to linger around like a stray cat waiting to be fed. God, why so much pain?

October of 2017, I attended the CCDA conference in Detroit. The last speaker of the conference was Gail Song Bantum. She spoke about how do you know what you are suppose do be doing. Basically, what is your purpose? She then said the four famous words which led me to begin my journey of walking in my purpose, "It's in your story". Really God? I need to share my story with other women like me? You really want me to let these people in my world?

The thought of people judging me based on my past frightened the pure crap out of me. Do you feel the same way? Well, guess what? Your pain and story have purpose. I encourage you to fully walk in it. God is such a gentleman. He does not allow you to endure all those trials and tribulations without having a plan and purpose behind them. Although my heart ached like a migraine over the split up with Trooper, I asked God to show me what to do with all that pain. I needed him to show me how to wait on the promises that he made to me. He was going to allow me to be loved and to love authentically. It would be done his way and in his timing of course. I no longer wanted to desire what my flesh wanted, but to desire those things that God desired for me.

Surrendering is so necessary. After you have surrendered, you can begin to desire after the things that God had already set up for you before you ever existed in your mother's wound. Recall Jeremiah 29:11 ESV again, "For I know the plans I have for you". You can make plans if you want, but in Proverbs 19:21 it says, many are the plans in the mind of man, but it is the purpose of the Lord that will stand. God has assigned something specifically for you to do, that only you can do. I encourage you to be ready to accept and adjust to anything that God has for you that is not on your personal agenda. You have to learn how to not be in control of everything, which can be very challenging, but you just need to trust the process.

Your process and my process will look and feel different; however the ending of the process will be the same. It will all glorify God. I highly recommend that you do not covet what anyone else has because you have no idea of what they had to endure to get to where they are. You should also not judge anyone based on how they look, talk, dress, etc. because each one of us have a story to tell.

I am so grateful to God for allowing me to share my story with so much confidence. A few years ago, I would have never thought that I would be writing a book. There is more to me than I realize. There is work for me to do and I will complete it all. No matter what comes, God is going to see me through and I must continue to trust him with all my heart. I will walk in my purpose and see myself as God sees me. Fierce and fearless.

I now would like to celebrate myself. I celebrate the fact that I did not give up although I cried almost everyday. I celebrate the fact that I encouraged myself on the days that no else did or could. I celebrate my relationship with God and finally finding real love. I celebrate self love. Now, you to take the time and do the same thing. Celebrate you! Take a few minutes and write down all the things that you wish to celebrate yourself for even if no one else does. Walk in your purpose girl, with boldness and confidence, because someone else is depending on you.

_____

_____

_____

_____

_____

_____

_____

Let me leave this side note for you: You shall reap the harvest God promised you. Take back what the devil stole from you. You shall recover it all if you faint not. Now walk into your inheritance with your bad self!!

Chapter 18

Waiting with Expectancy

The word process means a series of actions or steps taken in order to achieve a particular end. Being processed is not easy at all. When you say "yes" to God, get ready to endure some pain. Your salvation does not exempt you from it, but it will give you a different perspective. You will understand that this pain is necessary to get you where you need to go; therefore, do not fight or curse the process no matter how hard it gets. Do it with a good attitude knowing that in the end you will receive your promises and God will get the glory.

A promise is a declaration or assurance that one will do a particular thing or that a particular thing will happen. God is not a man that he shall repent or lie. He will stand on his promises. It is our duty to trust him and be obedient to what he tells us to do. I shared with you what my process was like for me. I had to surrender, be purged, develop a intimate relationship with God, discover and develop who I was, and begin to walk in my purpose. Throughout this process I have learned to be patient, how to pray daily, how to trust the process, and that God is faithful.

Your process may not look anything like mine, but know that you do need to be processed for your promise. What is it that your heart is desiring? Is it love? Is it a job? Is it children? Is it a husband? Whatever it is, do not give up on God. He will not let you down. It may not look like you want it to look, but it is exactly how God needs it to look in order to develop you into the person you need to be.

My desire is to be married some day to a man who will love me unconditionally. He will pray for me, encourage me, worship with me, support me, provide for me, and protect me. I have been praying for him for quite some time and I am in the process of waiting on this promise from God. And I wait with great expectations! God will exceed what we ask for or even think. His thoughts and ways are much higher than ours. He said I would have a second chance; therefore I will get a second chance. In those moments of doubt, he reassures me in Hebrews 10:23, when he tells me to hold fast to the confessions of my hope without wavering because he who promised is faithful. When my husband find me I will be working. I will be walking in my purpose, and most of all, I will be loving me.

Disappointments and doubt may come, but do not, I repeat, do not give up! Continue to do the things that God has called you to do. Be fearless and fierce. You are enough and you are worth waiting for. Stop selling yourself short. Release those past mistakes, have standards and do not settle just because you think that your biological clock is ticking away. Let's wait for the promises of God with hope, faith, a good attitude, and with great expectancy. It is my prayer that it will be sooner than you think. Now, get to work while you wait!

References

Holy Bible: English Standard Version. (2001). Wheaton, IL: Crossway Bibles.

Pinterest. (n.d.). Retrieved from https://www.pinterest.com/ Inspirationalquotes

www.ingramcontent.com/pod-product-compliance
Lightning Source LLC
Chambersburg PA
CBHW021154090426
42740CB00008B/1087